Presented to:

Leanne Neudorf

From:

Mom + Dad

Date:

Christmas 2008

Published by J. Countryman, a division of Thomas Nelson, Inc., Nashville, Tennessee 37214

Written by: Mark K. Gilroy
Managing editor: Jessica Inman

www.jcountryman.com
www.thomasnelson.com

Designed by Thinkpen Design LLC, Springdale, Arkansas

ISBN 1-4041-0358-9

Printed and bound in the United States of America

Pathways *of* Peace

SIMPLE WORDS *of* COMFORT *to* ENCOUNTER
GOD'S PRESENCE *in* THE MIDST *of* LIFE'S STORMS

Comfort in the Storm

INTRODUCTION

In every life there will be storms; those inevitable moments of uncertainty, turmoil, and strife.

God's gifts to His children—and you are His much loved child— are found in His words of comfort, strength, and insight that help you build bridges of love and face life with insight and poise. But the greatest gift of all is His very presence in your heart and life. He never leaves you nor forsakes you; God is always there for you.

Whether the sun is shining brightly or you are facing swirling winds and driving rain, experience God's comfort and guidance today as you follow His paths of peace.

Peace comes when there is
no cloud between us and God.
Peace is the consequence of forgiveness,
God's removal of that which obscures
His face and so breaks union with Him.

CHARLES H. BRENT

Peace comes
from being in
close relationship
with God—it is
His *gift* to us.

God's simple words to His children

when they are bombarded

with the cares of this world are,

"Be still and know that I am God."

There is a time for action, but first we

must stand and rest in His presence.

What worries you today?

What problems must you solve?

What must you get done?

Will you pause first for a moment

to quiet yourself before God?

God has not promised us
a life free from trouble and
challenges. But He has
promised us His presence
and strength. When you turn
to Him in total reliance and
trust, God's Spirit provides
you with a supernatural
freedom from worry,
anxiety, and fear.

11

To experience peace, you need not try harder, but simply trust more.

Trusting God offers greater peace than any worldly comfort—and enables you to find the confidence and strength you need by leaning your entire weight on God.

We wish and strive for God's most precious
gifts—peace, joy, forgiveness, and love—when
all along He has told us that we will find
these gifts only when we first seek Him.

If you would be happy and content,
don't race down the paths of pleasure
and human endeavor, though they make
such bold promises. Rather, simply ask God
to allow you to experience Him more fully.
Happiness and contentment will then
sneak up on you when you least expect it.

*Do not worry
about anything,
but pray and ask God
for everything you need,
always giving thanks.
And God's peace,
which is so great
we cannot understand it,
will keep your hearts
and minds in Christ Jesus.*

PHILIPPIANS 4:6-7

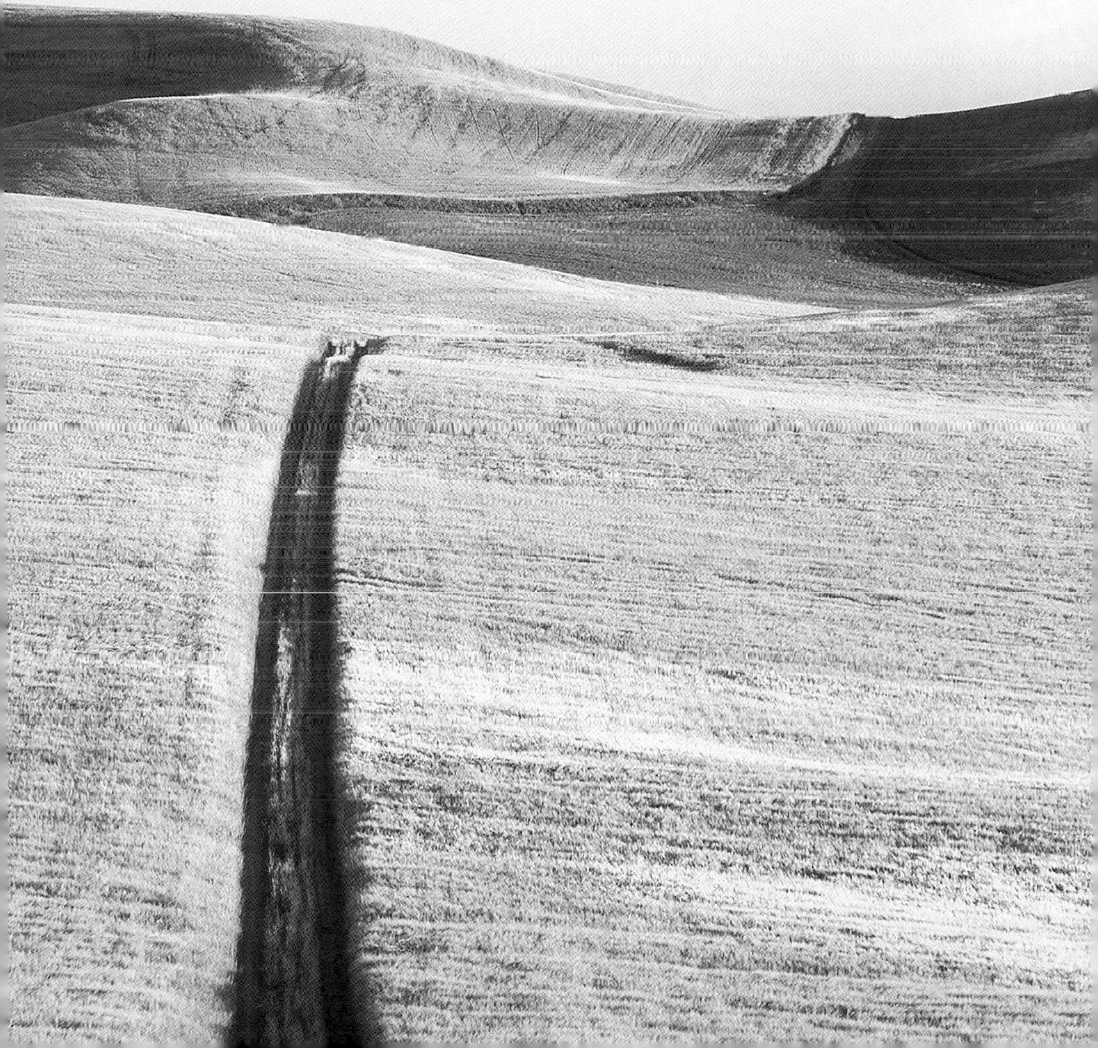

Get along with each other,

and forgive each other.

If someone does wrong to you,

forgive that person because

the Lord forgave you.

Colossians 3:13

Peace comes
with a spirit of
forgiveness—it is
a gift we extend
to others and that
always comes back
as a blessing
in our own lives.

Peace flows
between heaven
and earth when
we extend
the forgiveness
and mercy
we have received
from God
to both our friends
and enemies.

The first step to peace
between you and the one
with whom you have conflict
and brokenness—whether
friend, family, or true
adversary—is almost always
the most difficult step of all:
It is reaching toward the
other in humility, with
no guarantee they will
reach back in kind.

23

I was so fearful of what

I might lose in the process

of seeking reconciliation:

my reputation; my self pride;

perhaps most of all,

my adamant claims of being

the one who was right all along.

When I finally forsook such willfulness

and simply obeyed God, I found I had

lost nothing at all, and gained a sweet peace

I could never have experienced any other way.

Have you held onto a grudge? A slight from years ago?
A painful event from your childhood or recent past?

Though your claims of mistreatment may be well justified,
just think about what God could do in your heart and life
if you were to let go today, yea even this very hour.

God doesn't change the world through the life of one
who is stingy with grace, but through the one who
shares grace in the measure it has been received.

Forgive us for our sins,
just as we have forgiven those
who sinned against us.

MATTHEW 6:12

The Christian faith is meant to be lived
moment by moment. It isn't some broad,
general outline—it's a long walk with a real Person.
Details count: passing thoughts, small sacrifices,
a few encouraging words, little acts of kindness,
brief victories over nagging sins.

JONI EARECKSON TADA

Peace is a lifestyle—
a fruit of how
we *walk* and
how we *talk*.

Some paths that promise peace
are in reality gateways to strife.

Give a child anything he asks for and never say no
to him, and in so doing create a breeding ground
for a lifetime of unrest and complaint.

Likewise, never say no to yourself, and belatedly
discover that self-indulgence does not deliver
its promise of contentment and satisfaction,
but rather fosters the twisted desires
known as greed and lust.

Don't trade the trust
you have earned
with loved ones
for fleeting pleasure
or temporal gain.
Peace comes from
loving relationships,
and loving relationships
are always built on trust.

In the noise and confusion
of our fast-paced, busy world,
the quiet voice of peace
can only be heard when
we choose silence.

It was only after his years
in the desert that Moses led
his people to freedom.
If Jesus chose to step away
from the crowds and be alone
for prayer, how much greater
is our need for such solitude.

A soft answer

turns away wrath,

But a harsh word

stirs up anger.

PROVERBS 15:1 NKJV

I would rather be what God chose to make me
than the most glorious creature I could think of;
for to have been thought about, born in God's thought,
and then made by God, is the dearest, grandest,
and most precious thing in all thinking.

GEORGE MACDONALD

We experience a profound *peace* when we know and celebrate who we are in God's love and by loving ourselves.

Is it possible that we've made life too complicated, particularly when it comes to our relationships?

What is it that we all truly want—and deep down most need? Isn't it simply to love and to be loved?

And mightn't the giving and receiving of love be found in a quiet walk in the woods with your family? An agenda-free afternoon of talking—and not talking—with your beloved? Less volume and kinder words? More listening? A hand-written note? A hug or touch that takes just a second or two longer? A Monday night of games, pizza, and no TV?

Peace might be closer and simpler than we know.

Ambition and
a healthy desire
for self-improvement
have their place in life.
But the way of peace
means we believe God
when He tells us
He loves us just
the way we are.

Ah, the joy and peace of finding
that sweet spot in life where we
love others and receive love
freely without the rancor of
competition and comparison.

In your desire for achievement
and rewards and significance in
life, first walk down the path
of knowing that the One who
created you and who knows
your heart is the same One who
loves you most. And He has a
purpose and plan for your life.

Certainly we need goals

and dreams to fuel

our existence, but just

as importantly—nay,

more importantly—

we need to be part

of a fellowship of trust,

acceptance, and love.

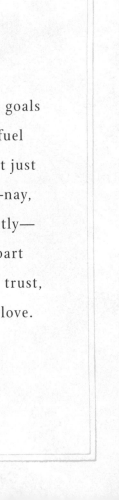

I discovered that I couldn't truly love and
affirm others until I first loved and affirmed myself.

Jealousy of his accomplishments ... an acute desire
to put her in her place ... a secret glee when misfortune
befalls him ... a quick readiness to partake of gossip
and rumors about her ... such feelings and attitudes
of harshness and judgmentalism sound an alarm in your
heart to care for the nourishment of your own soul.

Do you know where your
fights and arguments
come from? They come
from the selfish desires
that war within you.

JAMES 4:1

Often times God demonstrates

His faithfulness in adversity by providing

for us what we need to survive.

He does not change our painful circumstances.

He sustains us through them.

CHARLES STANLEY

When all else fails,
peace is something
we experience internally,
above and beyond
difficult *circumstances*.

Even if countries are
at war and everyone
around you is in strife
and conflict, you can
still experience an
exquisite peace in
your innermost being.

Faith, hope, and love
transcend all circumstances,
great or small, grave or light,
difficult or easy.

"Rejoice in the Lord always, and again I say rejoice," were Paul's words from a dank, dark prison cell in Rome.

How could a man of advanced education, significant position, and substantial affluence find himself in a place of such dire circumstances and yet still rejoice?

Not all of God's miracles are material. Some of the amazing moments in human existence occur in the spiritual realm and reveal God's power to transform us into His likeness.

*We could never learn to be
brave and patient if there
were only joy in the world.*

HELEN KELLER

*My brothers and sisters, when
you have many kinds of troubles,
you should be full of joy, because
you know that these troubles test your
faith, and this will give you patience.
Let your patience show itself perfectly
in what you do. Then you will be
perfect and complete and will
have everything you need.*

JAMES 1:2-4

Peace comes when you share from your bounty
with those in need ... when you freely and sincerely
rejoice with those who are rejoicing ... when
you offer friendship and presence to the
forgotten and lonely ... when you weep
with those who are heartbroken ... when you
offer the message of God's love in Jesus Christ
to those who are lost in sin ...

Peace comes when you see and love the world
as God sees and loves the world.

Yes, I am sure that neither death,
nor life, nor angels, nor ruling spirits,
nothing now, nothing in the future,
no powers, nothing above us,
nothing below us, nor anything else
in the whole world will ever be able
to separate us from the love of God
that is in Christ Jesus our Lord.

ROMANS 8:38-39

*I don't know what your destiny
will be, but one thing I do know:
The only ones among you who
will be really happy are those who
have sought and found how to serve.*

ALBERT SCHWEITZER

Peace goes
hand-in-hand
with *service*
to others.

Serving enables us
to put ourselves—and
our worries—aside
while we care for
the needs of others.

If you would be happy, strive to help
someone else find happiness. Caring for the needs
and concerns of others fosters a joy that focusing
all your energies and attentions on only yourself
can never deliver. And with that joy comes
deep, rich contentment and peace.

I leave you peace; my peace I give you.
I do not give it to you as the world does.
So don't let your hearts be troubled or afraid.

JOHN 14:27

Dear Heavenly Father,

Thank You so much for Your gift of peace.
Whether my life is bathed in sunlight or buffeted by
thunder storms, help me to always draw close to You
with love and gratitude.

Lord, I worship and praise You today. I lift my
fears and anxieties to You knowing that You lavish
peace on Your children. Thank You, Lord, for being
all I need—and so much more.

Amen.

For the past 12 years, Green Hill Productions has been the leader in creating music from quality instrumentals to exclusive compilations of legendary artists for all of our customers to enjoy. To find out more about our products or to locate a store near you, contact us at 1 (800) 972-5900 or check us out on the internet at www.greenhillmusic.com. Thanks to our valued partnership with Thomas Nelson, it is a pleasure to offer our music for your listening pleasure. Enjoy and have an inspiring read!

Sam Levine has given color and expression to a wide variety of artists' tracks, including Amy Grant, the Neville Brothers, Vince Gill and Michael McDonald.

Sam has more than 10 artist CD's in the smooth jazz and contemporary Christian genres. He has been nominated three times for a Dove Award and played on at least two Grammy Award winning recordings.

Sam continues to be an active studio musician, but he also leads a band called "City Lights" that is popular for wedding receptions and business conventions.

Violinist **David Davidson** has performed around the world as concertmaster, soloist, and chamber musician. Currently, David is the concertmaster of The Tennessee Summer Symphony and The Nashville Chamber Orchestra. He's also a member of The Nashville String Machine, the prestigious studio orchestra that records for the most major artists in the Nashville music community.

David's passionate violin playing can be heard on the hugely successful hymns projects by Michael W. Smith and recordings by Twila Paris and Third Day.

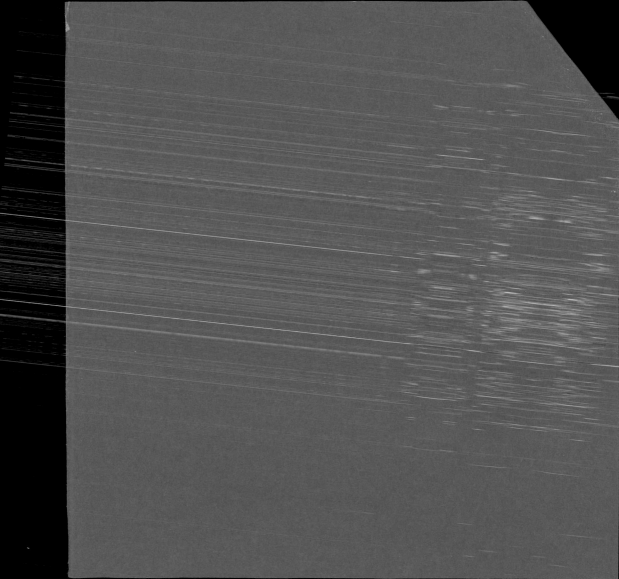